The Long Afternoon

The Long Afternoon

by John Kollock

Copple House Books   Lakemont, Georgia 30552
Distributed by Caroline House

Printed in the United States

Standard Book Number 0-932298-01-X

To my friend Henry Jarrell
who was for many years my
link with the past
and in memory
of his son
Carlton

Between Showers
From the collection of Jim Thacker

The lingering afternoons of late summer have a special charm. After the burning heat of midday, with our struggles to finish our work in spite of the temperature, the sun passes the peak of its power, and the day seems to slip into an endless tranquility of long shadows, katydids, and leisure. There seems to be time enough for anything; time to read, time to talk things over, time to visit, time to remember. It is as if there is a permanence in this golden period that makes life stand still, as if the day will never end. We are tempted to say, "This is it, this is the world as it should be; we have arrived at the best of all times, and it will go on forever." Of course, it does not. Sunset comes, and a touch of mist rises on the creek banks to hide the skimming waterbugs from the darting swallows. Strangely enough, within our memories, that happy interval is fixed forever, somewhere this side of evening.

There was a time when the rural countryside of much of our South was held fast in much the same way. Progress, industry, and world history seemed to happen elsewhere. In 1865, farming communities were left to their own devices, and a life style developed which is revealed to us in old photographs, letters, and memories.

By the turn of the century, rural families felt comfortable with their traditions, and few people ever traveled far from their places of birth. An occasional son or daughter left the farm and went to the "big city." But for this narrative, let us concern ourselves with those who did not leave home. Their histories are remembered only by surviving relatives. They were people who worked hard, played hard, worshipped devoutly, and believed in their world. They had a close relationship with the elements about them and a deep understanding of their Maker. There was strength in the family, sharing among neighbors, spiritual faith in God's powers, and a hope for better times tomorrow. The end of the world was coming as foretold in Revelations, not when the fossil fuels gave out or when someone dropped a bomb more awesome than the mind could grasp.

It was the age of the long afternoon. And this is how it was lived.

Nestled under the solid canopy of old oaks the shape of the farmhouse is barely visible. From the highway, that shape may be all you can see. The rest is a jumble of bushes and second growth trees that seem bent on engulfing the structure. A little distance from the house, a barn roof stands gaunt and grey against the horizon. In a moment you have flashed on down the highway and the image flickers out of your mind. Few travelers would think of seeking to find what might lie hidden in that thicket. To one familiar with evidences of the past, the exploration would tell a story as clearly as if the long departed owners were there to give their own accounting.

A good stout barn, for instance, was seldom torn down. If there was a new need for space, the building was simply modified to suit the purpose. By this process the older building gave birth to generations of sheds and lean-tos that wandered aimlessly about, scrambling up hills, or tucking themselves under the parent structure as the contour of the land demanded. The oldest section was the log structure, possibly only two cribs divided by a central hall. The switch to the use of sawed planks indicated a passage of time. Standing within a building still covered by shingles one might be struck by the amount of daylight showing through the dry cracks, but with the first falling rain the wood swells tight and the roof is quite waterproof.

13

Many old deserted barns still contain the remains of the family wagon wrapped in the shadows and cobwebs of yesterday. The average family used the wagon for every need; hauling hay in the summer, fertilizer in the spring, and the whole family all year round.

For the driver, there was a seat supported by large iron springs which took many of the teeth-rattling jolts out of the journey. If Grandma went to town, she sat in a special rump-sprung cane bottomed chair with the legs cut short. Those who were unable to fit on the driver's seat had to travel perched cautiously on the side boards, watching for the rough spots in the road so they could quickly stand and preserve their tailbones. The best part of the ride was on the river roads where the route was sandy for a mile or two, and they could sit on the tailgate and dangle their feet.

Because of constant usage, almost every part of the wagon was eventually patched in some way. Floorboards, side rails, tongues decayed or rotted. The wooden brake shoes were most often in need of rebushing as they were ridden hard on any long downhill stretch. Otherwise the team panicked, as the wagon crowded in on them, and a runaway might ensue. The trip home usually took a little less time. Something about heading back to the barn put a lot more life into a pair of plodding mules than any amount of flicking their backsides with the reins could on the trip out.

15

The workaday world of the small farm was divided into chores. Everyone had them, from the youngest to the eldest, and each learned to feel an individual sense of responsibility. If a small boy's task was to milk the family cow, and he failed in his duty, along about dark the bellowing from the barn would betray him.

The overall purpose was to keep the farm producing what was needed for survival and a little bit over for selling and trading. The growing seasons and their accompanying weather dictated the order of activities. It was important for a farmer to be able to predict weather with some accuracy, whether his prognosis was based on old signs, the almanac, or how his bad knee felt when he ventured forth to the outhouse. If he had a fair average in predicting, he became a sage and others adopted his system. Such familiar rhymes as, "When the dew is on the grass, rain will never come to pass" had a basis of truth.

When thinking of the chances the farmer took in risking his season's work on these simple sayings it is evident that he truly believed in the signs.

Checking The Signs

Main crops were planted in the large bottom land fields. By mid-summer the heat was intense. Nothing moved in the heavy air except the insects which seemed to thrive on the weather and the people trying to work in it. To a young boy it seemed he would have to follow forever the tail end of the family mule down the "longest furrows in the world" toward the distant haze of the far woods.

Probably the main thing that made field work bearable was the promise of spring water. Like an oasis in the desert, the spring place represented a haven of delight to those who took time from their chores and sought the fern covered shadows. There was usually a dipper or mason jar handy, but it was more fun to flop belly down at the edge of the basin and drink puppy fashion, pausing to study the cool depths of the water for signs of crawfish or salamanders. The fresh water came bubbling up from the sandy bottom making tiny volcanic eruptions that had a slightly hypnotic effect on the observer. And the water was COLD—icy cold. For some reason, it had a flavor that was almost sweet.

At dinner time the workers lingered on the bank and let their meal settle while the breeze that never seemed to reach the middle of the field, stirred in the trees overhead. Just as the world seemed perfect, someone would break the spell by heading back to work, and everyone would have to trudge reluctantly out into the blistering afternoon sun.

There was a saying, "when the weather wasn't fit for nothing else, you could still chop wood," and winter or summer, there was a never ending demand for fuel.

The wood shed near the house was in constant use, as the fire in the kitchen stove rarely stopped burning. There was water to heat, bread to bake, and a kettle of soup simmering the day long on the back eye.

There were preferences in the kinds of wood to cut and burn. Oak was chosen for slow fires and pine for quick, hot ones. Chestnut was not used for firewood as it was the best choice for fence rails.

In wet weather, when the wagons sank to their axles in the ruts, the one-horse farm sled brought logs in from a distance. Mud or no mud, firewood was a necessity as it was the primary source of energy.

Wash day began early in the morning so that the work around the huge iron pot was finished before the additional heat of the sun made work unbearable. The noise of beating the dirt out of the helpless clothes with a battling stick made the hills resound. No fragile material could hope to survive this treatment. Sometimes, the buttons were removed and sewn back on after the wash was over. Fortunately, there were no zippers, snaps or plastic parts, for they would have been destroyed.

When the wash was done, the girls draped the various garments and linen across the handy bushes in the yard. If necessary, they also used the brambles in the pasture. The effect was quite decorative, as if someone were trying to slipcover the countryside.

In the fall, when sumacs and sourwoods were brilliant red against the yellow and brown of the woods, it was syrup-making time. Around the mill a smell of overpowering sweetness rose on the crisp air, a smell that foretold many meals of syrup on cornbread and biscuits.

When the sorghum cane had been stripped and carried in from the fields, the mule was hitched to the "sweep" and was marched in a slow circle to power the mill as the cane was inserted between the rollers. The raw juice ran through a pipe to the boiler box or was drained through cheese cloth into a barrel for "toting" to the boiler.

Here for some hours the juice simmered and the dark skum that rose to the surface was skimmed off and thrown in the "skum pit." When the syrup had finished making, the corn cob plug was pulled and a thin stream of gold poured into the waiting jugs.

Syrup making was a hot, tiring and tedious chore which caused one weather-beaten mountain man to remark, "It's the closest I ever come to real work."

No farm could survive without the garden patch. It was the source of most of the summer eating and winter canned goods. Thus, spring planting was a long awaited activity. As the winter supply of canned goods dwindled and the empty jars outnumbered the full ones, evenings were spent reading seed catalogs and consulting the frayed copy of the almanac for signs for planting. Good Friday was the generally accepted time to begin. As each tiny sprout appeared, it seemed to represent another sign of nature's rebirth.

As the plants grew, the never-ending battle with the weeds began. Daily, the whole family took time between other chores to pull a few. In time, the rewards appeared. Baskets full of vegetables descended on the kitchen and, with a sigh of pleasure mixed with anticipation of hard work ahead, the ladies brought out the canning jars again.

Not all of the farm's crops needed as careful attention as those in the garden. The wild blackberry bushes that straggled along the fence rows and spread across the abandoned pastures took care of themselves. The last cold spell in the spring was called "blackberry winter," because it usually came when the blackberry bushes were in full bloom, and the masses of small white flowers gave the landscape the appearance of a light snowfall.

"When blackberries are red they're green, and when they are black they're ripe." And when they were ripe they were ready to defend themselves from the small army of pickers sent to harvest. The canes were insidiously clever in their determination to protect their fruit. They pricked and clawed the hand that grasped for the best specimen. Only the puny ones were in easy reach. When the pickers dared to wade into the thicket, the thorny tentacles closed in behind and attacked from the rear. The blackberries were never alone in this battle, for there were also armies of chiggers ready to attack.

The compensation was in eating while picking. Smaller children were always able to fill their stomachs but never their berry buckets. Then invariably they would be taken with a fit of the wearies mixed with other symptoms that could be claimed but not disproved at the moment. This would take them from the field of battle and into the shade. Somehow the others had to work on until the buckets were filled. Then there was the rush home to scrub down in cold water and strong soap that hopefully washed away the loose chiggers before they dug in.

29

"You eat what you can, and what you can't eat you can," or preserve or pickle or dry—or in some way put by for the time when nothing is coming in fresh. Every season of harvesting had its surplus that had to be put up. When the blackberries were finished, there were peaches and apples to peel and cut. For a while it was fun and many hands joined in willingly. But as the endless baskets were brought in, enthusiasm waned.

At last the bounty of the season filled the pantry shelves and the racks in the cellar. To keepers of the kitchen there was satisfaction in knowing that, months later, when the winter landscape was grim and grey, the taste of summer would still be fresh.

Out Back
From the collection of Ed and Angel Stewart

Gathering wild honey was a tricky business. But the honey was free and only cost the effort to go after it. Finding a bee tree required patience, as the bees had to be spotted as they gathered pollen from the flowers and tracked to their home. Once a bee tree was found, it was marked by its finder, and regardless of its location, it was his for the robbing.

Usually the tree had to be felled and split open and the honey scooped out, comb, bees and all. Even if the hive was smoked, there were plenty of mad bees around, but for some reason, a good bee man rarely got stung.

While gathering one of the few sweeteners available, a boy might take a honey fit and eat himself sick on handfuls of dripping comb, before the sticky wash tub of sweetness was toted home.

When evening came, the cows began their slow march to the milking hall. Sometimes they had to be driven from the fields or creek
banks.

In the milking hall there were mingled aromas of fresh hay,
cottonseed meal, and the cows themselves. Milkers chatted and fussed
with their charges as the sounds in the milk pails changed from a
hollow splat to a rich thick gurgle. A reluctant or restless cow received
a nudge in the side and a few choice words, but generally there was a
sense of tranquility in the hall.

Leftover milk found its way to the table in fat pats of butter
stamped with familiar designs from a wooden mold and buttermilk
came from the bottom of the churn. Dish clabber appeared after an
aging period. All in all, the family cows gave more than enough to
warrant their bit of pasture and the daily attention to their needs.

The fortunate farmer in the community who had falling water on his land usually elected to construct and operate a mill on a part-time basis. The building was tiny, with just room enough for the miller, the mill, and a spare meal bin to house the mill owner's toll. Payment was normally made in kind, since cash money was used only for store bought goods and for paying taxes.

Water from a small stream was trapped behind a dam and sent through a raceway to the mill. There it fell in a boxed wooden trough onto a horizontal wheel under the building. This tub wheel (with its baffles) was often cut from a single slice of tree trunk. As long as it stayed fairly wet, it would last; if left to dry, it would rot.

The actual grinding did not take long, but farmers extended the waiting period by swapping stories and bits of news. Since visits to the mill were so frequent "a body didn't want for company."

Not every farm was set up with a complete blacksmith shop, but someone was usually available within walking distance to serve his neighbors. Horseshoes, hinges, plowshares, wagon parts, and even cowbells were fasioned from bits and pieces of scrap that surrounded the shed. Nothing was ever tossed away, and the quality of the metal was such that items seldom rusted. A wagon might eventually fall apart if allowed to stand in the weather, but the parts were recycled to repair other vehicles. Clever smiths modified old mule shoes into brackets for pole gates, bits of broken trace chain into latches, and spare buggy wrenches were made into elegant door handles.

The variety of craft work in a community was usually related to daily needs, and there was little time for making things "just for pretty." There could be beauty in handcrafted objects, but they were basically utilitarian.

Jug makers, for example, provided containers for carrying and storing many of the family necessities. The raw materials had to be close at hand to set up a jug mill, so the operation was located near a clay supply. Once the clay had been ground and wedged, the potter settled himself in his little shed at the primitive kick wheel. Here, by the hour, he fashioned the simple shapes. Eventually, he and his work-room took on the look of a dirt dauber's nest, with a film of white clay dust over everything. While the pots dried, the potter ground the glazes in a primitive quern made of two stones fitted into each other. Glazes were then painted on the greenware, and they were ready for firing in a beehive kiln. Firing was more a matter of instinct than science. The resulting pots could be a mixture of excellence, accept-ability, and total disaster.

43

To the isolated farm family the peddler and his pack were a welcome sight. He brought news as well as his wares. As time passed, his stock increased and his pack evolved into a rolling store. His wagon seemed to burst with exciting merchandise, and his rapid patter brought an element of carnival life. Housewares were tempting to women customers, and the patent medicines and other cures were always popular items. A heavy percentage of alcohol was the base for many of the medicines so that at least a temporary cure was effected, giving the peddler a change to rattle off over the ridge.

The country doctor was a constant traveler in all seasons and in all weather. His equipment was crammed into a battered black satchel. His operating room might be a porch step, the family bedroom or the kitchen table. He never know whether the next visit would be to patch a cut, deliver a baby, or set a broken leg with all of the family gathered around to help and observe.

There were few hospitals, and nursing was done by the family or nearby neighbors. In time the doctor came to blend his formal education with the superstitions which some of the old folks held dear. It was wiser to go along with a belief, rather than to upset the patient. An ax driven in the floor or a knife under the bed to "cut the pain" could do no harm.

Herbs and natural cures were part of the doctor's medical supplies. He might cultivate plants he needed in his practice around his home.

Often, the only payment the patients could make was produce, and the floor of the doctor's buggy was filled with vegetables, eggs and the like on his return home. People paid what they could and when they could, and seldom, if ever, was a sick person refused help. Debt paying was a matter of honor, and only a trifling person would want to be beholden, especially to one as beloved as the doctor.

Home Stretch

The crossroads store, like the tub mill, served the community's daily needs. It usually did not have a large stock, but the arrangement and clutter made it seem as if there was a little bit of everything tucked somewhere back in the dark cobwebed corners.

If the storekeeper handled the mail, the center of activity was the post office. People had to check their pigeon holes to see if there was a post card, letter, catalogue or weekly paper, and this was a fine excuse for a trip to the store. Then, of course, they had to pass the time of day and exchange the local gossip. In winter it was nice to linger around the warmth of the pot belly stove and predict the next snowstorm. The store was also the natural gathering place for the elderly who found companionship and a sense of being in on the activities of the world through exchanging opinions within aiming distance of the brass spittoon.

Saturday was town day. A list of household and personal needs was made during the week and when Saturday arrived, everyone was ready to go. Produce to sell or barter was loaded on the wagon. Most of the family wanted to make the trip even if they had nothing to do except to see who was on the square.

Once in town, the wagons were pulled off to the side of the general store and the mules tied with their heads in the shade of the overhanging trees. This trip was no frivolous spending spree. Staples, coal oil and other household good were carefully selected by the head of the kitchen. Men took care of the feed store supplies and admired new items in the hardware. Every male had a pocket knife which had to have its turn at the whetstone on the counter.

As the ladies lingered in the fascinating world of yard goods, the men-folk drifted back to the wagons to inspect and evaluate their neighbors' mules or horses. Quite often teams swapped traces during the afternoon.

On the trip home, Mother's mind was on the bolt of material resting carefully in her lap while the children savored the last of the hard candy they had bought as a special treat, and Father tried to decide whether he had gotten the best end of his trade.

The week that the circuit judge came to the county seat often turned into a combination carnival, street revival, horse-trading session, and picnic. Everything centered around the court house which at other times drew little attention. People came from miles around to join in the festivities. A line of volunteers perched on the rock wall in front of the court house, waiting to get a call to jury duty and the day's pay it afforded. The street preacher held forth in loud tones, while the traveling drummer sold his doodads to those with money.

In the summer, when the windows of the court room had to be propped open to allow enough ventilation for the survival of the occupants, the voices of the contending lawyers rang out into the hot summer air of the court yard. Here they mingled with the buzz of horseflies and voices of people talking about crops and weather. On such occasions, it was always easy to recognize the people running for office. They were the well scrubbed and Sunday-best-dressed individuals who went from group to group, pumping arms, exuding charm as well as the aroma of hair tonic.

As court week ended, the stately old building settled down for another month or so. The hound dogs reclaimed their rightful places in the shade of the trees, and someone collected the empty lunch sacks and chewing tobacco wrappers that drifted to rest against the building.

Just Plain Winter
From the collection of Dr. and Mrs. Philip Z. Israel

The general store in the village was the big brother of the cross-roads store. Here the shelves seemed to hold everything that one could ever desire from bare necessities to luxuries beyond the means of many. In addition the store was the setting for checker contests, political debates, and discussions on almost any subject.

It was also the hub of communication, passed by word of mouth or over the telephone. The only public phone in town might be located in one corner of the store. Private conversation was quite impossible, as it was usually necessary to screech loudly to be heard over the miles of swagging wires. Hearing was equally difficult, as the conversation was interspersed with crackling sounds and a dull roar that made the voice of the other party seem to come from a deep whirlpool into which he might sink from hearing at any moment.

Whatever news a person received was heard by everyone in the store before he hung up. It was also heard by most of the people along the party line, because when one phone rang, they all rang. The number of rings indicated for whom the call was intended, but usually everyone picked up. After all, there were not that many calls coming through. Then too, some people could hear better than others, and if the message was not understood by the party for whom it was intended, his neighbors filled him in on the details.

The activities at the railroad station were an important part of daily life. The quiet village atmosphere was shattered by the sound of the whistle as the train rounded the bend and steamed into the valley. Departing passengers scrambled for their bags and stray children. The station master took command of the platform like the captain of a ship. The coming and going of the trains was a grand entertainment for the children. They lined the banks to wave, as the noisy giant hissed and screeched to a halt. Cinders drifted into the hair and eyes of onlookers.

Once the train had paused, there was a flurry of movement as freight was loaded and lumpy mail bags were tossed onto the wooden deck. The conductor kept up the fever pitch by hustling everyone off and on as quickly as possible. Trying to keep on schedule, he would give several nervous glances at his huge pocket watch; this was impressive in a community where sunrise and sunset were the usual framework for accomplishments.

Clouds of steam engulfed the depot as the departing engine made its noisy adjustments. The ear shattering whistle sent chills up many spines and scattered the pigeons. The big brass bell on the engine clanged, the drive shafts flexed like giant grasshopper legs and the wheels began to roll. Passengers shouted goodbyes from the windows, the conductor bellowed, "All aboard," although he could see that everyone was aboard. And the train rumbled off into the pasture land leaving only a trail of black smoke to drift across the landscape. The town was quiet once more.

The photographic studio did much to preserve the images of the past for future generations. It was an important day when the family gathered in the fascinating world of the photographer.

In his cluttered room were objects strange and wonderful to behold. Sunlight flooded through a huge glass window, and all about were fancy armchairs, flower urns and pedestals, toy boats in the shape of swans, velour drapes tied back with gold cords, and an assortment of background scenes on shade rollers that transported subjects to exotic locations.

The camera itself was a formidable device, which due to its size and curious shape commanded respect. The black drape that hung over it had an ominous air that gave one the feeling that the object was in mourning and should not be disturbed.

The photographer needed to be both a saint and a diplomat. Often his subjects were children, and the need to keep them still long enough for a proper exposure proved to be quite a task. One invention for managing this was a chair with a hole in the back through which the parent got an unseen grip on the squirming infant and held him like a ventriloquist's dummy. For older models, there were stands that locked the head in a wire clamp to prevent movement. In the resulting photograph a person had a somewhat rigid appearance, as if he had a gun in his back.

"Watching the birdie" in the camera lens was the most popular way to be photographed. This produced a full-face picture with a somewhat glazed look as if the subject were in trance. If there was an expression of strained frustration, it might have come from an inability to see neither hide nor hair of the "birdie" in the little glass window. Regardless of the outcome, the pictures became prized possessions and were given a place of honor in the home.

Morning Coffee

There were several degrees of washing up on the farm. On the wash porch outside the kitchen at the back of the house, a basin, a bit of homemade soap, and a bucket of well water stood ready for a quick clean up when yard work was done. In the evening after working in the dusty fields, there was a tin wash tub to scrub tired feet in and clean the layers of redness away, thus saving the bed sheets from ruin. In winter these operations were moved into the kitchen.

The ritual of the full bath took place generally once a week. There was very little room in a tin tub for bathing, and no room for modesty. Several people had to use the same bath water until it cooled off. Mothers used lye soap and a bristle brush to be sure that certain areas were properly scrubbed. It would never do to let the children go to Sunday Meeting and present a dirty neck to the neighbors in the pew behind.

Going to bed on Saturday night with a clean body and clean sheets gave one a strangely exhilarating feeling, as if many sins had already been washed away without even setting foot in the church.

67

The reward for suffering the misery of scratchy, starched shirts and tight shoes during Meeting time, was the prospect of Sunday dinner. On this special day, if times were good, the table was overflowing with food. If a son or daughter were home for a visit, their particular favorites were added to the fare. The prayers were longer, of course, but it was the Lord's day and he deserved the thanks and praise. Drop in visitors were simply squeezed in. Somehow an extra place or so could always be set between the high chair and the maiden aunt. It was a good feeling to be able to share with those who might not be as fortunate.

When the table was empty and the family filled, they went to sit in the rockers lined up in the deep shade of the front porch and visit. Guests might linger on until evening enjoying the day of rest. When the children began to dart about catching lightning bugs it was time to call it a day.

In many rural communities church was not held every Sunday, and Meeting Day was special. Morning service was followed by dinner on the grounds, an eagerly awaited feast. The request to "bring a covered dish" brought out the competitive spirit in a woman.

Families loaded their wagons carefully for the journey to the church grounds. Pots of vegetables were placed on the floor of the buggy and steadied so they did not slosh over. A fancy cake usually rode in the lap of the lady who prepared it, so that no damage would occur before it was presented to the admiring congregation. In addition to the delicious fried chicken, ham and many other tempting foods, each family who came to the gathering brought plates, serving silver, and their best table cloth. Of course, the table cloths never matched, but they made a splendid confusion of designs on the rough wooden tables in the side yard. Only the old people were provided with chairs, usually brought from home. Everyone else stood up at the tables or perched on a rock or stump. Moving about made it possible to eat more, and no one wanted to miss at least a taste of the best each household had to offer. Fresh spring water and lemonade were consumed in great quantities, which kept a bucket brigade busy trudging back and forth to the spring.

The combination of food and fellowship was often followed by a lengthy session of gospel singing in the afternoon which filled the hearts and spirits even better than the chicken and apple pie had filled their stomachs.

Handiest Shed On The Place

Courting in days past was a traumatic affair. When a boy began to wash all over and experiment with violent smelling hair oils, it was a good sign that the sap was rising. Dirt disappeared from elbows which had not been seen since early childhood. Freckles were a country curse, but no amount of scrubbing with lye soap could cause them to disappear.

A girl had the advantage in liking to dress up and do interesting things with her hair. After all, she had been looking forward to courting since early childhood. The poor boy meanwhile, had devoted most of his attention to fishing and hunting. His hair had been used to keep his hat from slipping around. Now confronted with the pressing need to look his best, the easiest solution was to paste his locks against his skull and put on a brave front.

One evening he would hitch the plow mule for a ride across the valley, an overt act which was a clear sign of intent. The element of doubt as to how his presence would be received only added to the tension he experienced. Rocking in the squeaky porch swing, a couple might hold hands and steal a kiss, but they were always aware of many eyes and ears upon them. In the darkness the exotic mingling of odors of lilac water and hair pomade in the company of this strange new creature—whom he had probably known all his life—soon drove the poor boy to the extreme of "Popping the question." Once this step had been taken both families were able to get a little more sleep.

When a young couple stood up in church to take their vows, it was usually a joyous event for the whole community. If there was any apprehension, it was on the part of the groom who still looked with fear at this fateful step. After all, once you were hitched, you stayed hitched. Country families seldom thought of swapping mules half way down the field.

If the newlyweds farmed, as almost everyone did, the wedding meant a partnership in love and work as well. Ahead would be a lifetime of sharing chores and problems that befell the household. Husband, wife, and children would work their way together down the corn rows, chopping weeds, pulling fodder, harvesting, gardening and tending the stock.

There was a mixed blessing in all of this. It drew couples closer together over the years. At the end of the day as they sat on the porch overlooking the fresh greens in the garden patch or a new section of fence surrounding the barn yard, they could share their weariness, their joy in what they had accomplished, and a satisfaction in knowing that they really needed each other as partners in the life they shared.

Rural schools were only in session when the children were not needed to help on the farm. All ages attended, including adults who wanted book learning so they could read and write and cipher. They sat on rough wooden benches and did their sums and spelling on little slates with bits of chalk. Mothers usually sent a scrap of cloth with their children to clean their slates, but the boys preferred spitting on them and polishing them with a grubby shirtsleeve.

The children played in the dusty school yard at recess. There was no equipment provided, but if someone had a ball and a stout stick, they could get a game going. Most of the boys' pockets contained such treasures as string, a pocket knife, and one or two earthenware or glass marbles. Marbles was popular, but you had to be good or cautious with whom you played—most games were for "keepers."

If there was nothing else to do, the boys would arm wrestle, fight, chase each other, or think up a contest involving a test of strength.

The girls played house with acorns and sticks, or made clover chains to wear as necklaces or crowns. They also played singing games. Older girls might concentrate on getting the attention of the boys by teasing or acting aloof.

After recess when the students crowded back into the school room, the aroma of sweat and chalk dust would hang heavily on the air.

Hall Barn

The county fair was a long anticipated event. The dates were carefully noted on the frayed Farmer's Almanac calendar that hung in the kitchen. Everyone with any sense of competition looked forward to the time when his prize pig or giant pumpkin would be judged. Mountains of sweet cakes and pies emerged from busy kitchens. Quilts and other needlework were carefully packed for the trip. At last the little parades of wagons, buggies and buckboards began their journeys to the fair grounds. In the wake of the vehicles the proud menfolk and boys drove their stock, which had been groomed as carefully as the people themselves.

A good fair was designed to judge everything from bed quilts to brute strength. In this way a person's trade or special skill could be singled out and honored by his neighbors. Honored, perhaps, is the wrong word. Envied might be applicable, because the losers were more inclined to feel as green and sour as their best pickles.

When the fair days were over, the ride home might be unusually quiet as each savored the satisfaction of victory, or set his mind to do better next year.

Most farm yards had one or two rangy dogs that seemed to spend most of their days in a state of complete exhaustion, stretched out in the sun or lying in the shade of the porch floor. They rose to bark at strangers, and only after they had been duly commanded to hush, resumed their lethargic state. Their apparent lack of purpose was deceiving; these dogs were prized possessions of the men in the family—coon dogs, capable of boundless energy on the trail.

Coon hunting was a nocturnal activity, looked upon as a night out with the boys. Dogs and men gathered at dusk and headed off into the woods. When a suitable spot was located, they built a fire and let the dogs loose. As soon as the scent was struck, the melodious barking would begin. The pleasure was in listening to the dogs bugle and following the sounds of the chase. Each man knew the voice of his own hound. When the baying indicated the dogs had treed a racoon, the men took off toward that spot. They tried to dislodge the coon, even if it meant cutting down the tree. Once on the ground a coon would fight with the best of them, and a tough scrapper might win his freedom. But the cleverest ones escaped by jumping unnoticed into neighboring branches, and left the hunting party "barking up the wrong tree."

Music seemed to touch the heart of rural people. It was an artistic expression that came naturally to them. They were self-taught musicians, many of whom made their own instruments. Those who didn't play could sing along, and many an evening was spent picking and singing.

For high times, nothing beat gathering a group of friends for a hoe-down. With a good fiddler, a banjo man, and a guitarist playing together in the corner, it was a test of endurance between the dancers and the musicians.

The basic step of the old time dancing was a shuffling gait punctuated by rhythmic banging of the heels with great force, as if one were trying to knock off a clod of clay. In its old form, it was called "stomp dancing." The figures and patterns in the squares were complex and graceful, but the danger of being stomped by an extra enthusiastic dancer was ever present.

Country boys swam in their birthday suits. Few children owned a bathing costume, which was a rather unlovely thing to behold. The material was heavy and irritating wool which felt like long underwear made of scrubbing pads. It was much more fun to slip off from chores and plunge naked into the creek on a hot sticky afternoon.

Going swimming really meant jumping out of trees to see who could make the biggest splash or swinging on a rope to drop off in the deepest part. The actual swimming was confined to the dog padde, if the water was deep enough. Those who held back because they didn't think they could learn to swim, were simply tossed in the stream and quickly learned on the way back to shore.

As there were no towels handy for drying off, swimmers usually went home in a slightly damp condition which they hoped their parents would confuse with honest sweat.

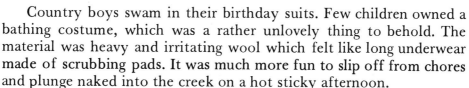

Shucking corn was an occasion for getting together to combine hard work and fun. By now most of the crops were harvested, and it was time for a change of pace. The early fall air felt so invigorating that everyone set about the job of stripping off the husks in a holiday mood.

There was a custom that if a boy found a red ear of corn, he won a kiss from the prettiest girl at the gathering. Of course, it was his say who she was. Occasionally the owner of the corn would hide a jug in the depths of the pile, and the one who got down to it first was the winner. He did not, however, win the whole jug, for it usually had to be passed around.

When the work was done, along about midnight, the whole group would turn to dancing and keep it up until morning light.

The quilting bee was strictly a ladies function and a happy one. The quilting frame was often set up in the parlor and it was as much a party as it was a work session. Whoever the quilt belonged to provided the meal for everyone.

Without the men around, they could talk about subjects of particular interest to the ladies. Family problems, love affairs, babies, all the forbidden fruits of mixed conversation, could be openly discussed. All went home from the day of quilting fully refreshed and brimming over with the latest news about life around the community.

The care and detail that was evident in the quilting was witness to the fact that no one was in a hurry to get done.

Hay rides were a popular group activity. They were enjoyed by all ages, but the young people had the most fun. All that was needed was a wagon full of sweet smelling hay and a slow team. Everyone piled in and there was singing and laughter as the wagon rumbled along the lane.

Perhaps the destination was a picnic spot and a few baskets of cold chicken and sandwiches were tucked under the driver's seat. The afternoon was filled with games and rough housing in the open meadows. The horses enjoyed the outing as much as the children. For them it meant grazing idly in the shade or standing in the cool of a stream with the water swirling against their hot shanks.

When the time came to go home, baskets and bodies were piled back into the hay. In contrast to the rowdy trip out, the return journey had a hazy glow of weariness to it. And if the driver nodded off, no one noticed, for the team knew the way home and they were unlikely to meet any traffic.

Making ice cream was an adventure requiring time and muscle, and the result was more than just another dessert. Young and old took turns cranking until the mixture became stiff. Small fingers fought for a sample as the dasher was removed. For some reason, this first taste was the best of all. Licking the dasher was frowned upon by the adults as unsanitary, and there was also the danger of splinters in the tongue.

After repacking the cylinder in the briny ice, the family anxiously waited for the creamy contents to "set up," while watching the road for the kinfolk who invariable came calling on such occasions. Cousins always seemed to eat more than their share of homemade ice cream.

Second Flurry

Snow in the south was not frequent or long lived enough to become boring. The first white blanket of flakes was regarded as a surprise party by the young. On that grey morning when the familiar barns and sheds were decked in white and the pastures and wood lands seemed strangely different, there was a burst of activity.

Extra scarves and mittens were dug from cedar chests, and barn lofts ransacked for homemade sleds and rusty skates. The snow was carefully tested for its snowball making ability. If it was satisfactory, a fight resulted. Afterwards, the whole gamut of winter games was explored. The best slopes were converted from a smooth white blanket into a network of crisscrossed tracks and boot prints. Snow angels were created by children lying on their backs in the snow and flapping their arms.

When the cold lasted long enough to freeze the small ponds, there were skating parties and bonfires. But all too soon, the sun broke through the overcast and the south slopes became slushy with patches of red clay. Then the snow was gone, and it was just plain winter again.

99

Christmas on the farm was a festive time, full of anticipation and excitement. Gifts were neither numerous nor fancy, but carefully planned for each individual. There were many secret projects; Mother knitted a new sweater to replace the one with the worn elbows, Grandfather built a sled in the barn, and sister created a doll from scraps of leftover materials. There was a wonderful spirit of wanting to give, and wanting to please someone in a special way, to show them how much they were loved.

A carefully selected tree was brought in from the woods, and trimmings fashioned around the kitchen table in the evening. The children heard the story of the first Christmas read from the family Bible, and donkeys and stables took on a new meaning.

On Christmas morning, gifts were exchanged and each gave and received his little bit of thoughtfulness. But the greatest gift that was shared was love, for this lasted a lifetime.

Between the very young and very old there can be a special bond of understanding and appreciation. It is as if the younger one is saying, "Look at the world with me and see how wonderful it all is in each tiny aspect of its creation and growth. Come share it with me, for I need a companion who will understand and feel the wonder, even if we can only communicate with the touch of our hands or the warmth of our bodies as you hold me up to grasp a budding limb."

The older companion may silently respond, "Now I understand what life is all about. It is not what we are or have become, for that is passing. It is the glory of God's world, His world that we have been allowed to dwell in. How many sunsets have we missed in the pursuit of our desires? How many spring flowers, miraculous in creation and beauty, have we crushed on the path toward our fortunes? Now let me sit in the warmth of the sunshine and impart this wisdom to you."

The child can grasp the meaning, because he sees the beauty of dewdrops in the morning garden and runs to feel the wind in his face.

We seemed to hold on to life's wonder longer in those days. With several generations under one roof, there was a mingling of ideas, and each segment made valuable contributions. Even in old age a person continued to serve in some capacity. Grandma might only sit and snap beans, but she did it long and well. The sense of being a part of family life kept her spirit bright. And when she no longer occupied the little rocker by the window, there was a vacant space in the hearts of the family that could not be filled.

103

When the long afternoon is over, there comes a time between sunset and darkness we call afterglow.

The light of today has gone over the ridge to stir others to action, and we are left in a moment of seeing and understanding that has a dreamlike quality. The things about us become more dear because in a few moments they will vanish into darkness. There are those who would shun this time of day as too sentimental; they would turn on the lights and rush to create a false day inside the house, as if they feared the night.

But wait a bit. Don't light the lamp. For just a moment look at what has passed. It has a beauty now in this strange other light. The edges of remembered hardships have lost their sharpness. Although the form of the world we know is still before us, it has mellowed into a glowing oneness that holds no grief.

Afterglow
From the collection of Dr. and Mrs. Joseph V. Morrison Jr.

The long afternoon is over, and now the afterglow is fading, too. Let us pick up the good things we remember that lie scattered about like so many toys, and carry them in our minds into the house, for they may come in handy in the morning light.

Acknowledgements

In order to thank all of those who contributed to this book, I will have to go back more than ten years. In the fall of 1967, my friend Glenn Summerlin, president of Grizzard Advertising in Atlanta, asked me to design a set of prints about rural life as a Christmas offering for his clients. I was pleased with the assignment because it was in line with my interests and the painting I was doing.

I researched the subject matter and used as backgrounds the buildings and scenery I had known as a boy. I talked with friends and relatives who had been involved in their youth with many of the events I wished to depict. From the details they remembered, I began to piece together a patchwork of images that were incorporated into the final drawings. The prints were well received, and I continued to do four a year for the next ten years. They were called "Down Home" prints.

Each year work began in August when I had decided on the four themes, and when we had a maximum number of visitors on our farm who could be lured from the shade of the porch to participate in a dress-up activity.

Friends, their children and, of course, my family would costume themselves from the piles of garments brought down from our barn loft. That is our repository for ancestral trunks, costumes and high school graduation gowns. Next the props would be collected and the cast would prepare to pose in the appropriate setting. Then with the camera loaded with fast film, we would begin.

Fortunately, from the beginning, we had a core of uninhibited performers. Inspired by their enthusiasm, those of lesser experience or courage were swept into the action. The scene would be set—"You are in a school yard . . . at recess . . . you are playing games . . . what sort of games did they play then . . . —let's play marbles . . . ."

George Williams and his family were part of almost all of the prints. George has dramatic ability developed during many years of performing and directing Gilbert and Sullivan operettas at the University where he is a professor. For example, the delight on the faces of the guests in the wedding print was not a response to the happy event they were witnessing, but to Mr. Williams' hilarious portrayal of the minister.

Young Harriet Williams has the ability to seize on the mood of the moment and carry all of those around her into the action. One very hot day the subject was "winter fun." A dozen adults and children roasting in wool jackets, scarfs and knit caps, followed Harriet's lead, skated and cracked the whip on the green lawn, built imaginary snow men and even huddled around a brush fire. Another day, while portraying a student who had forgotten her lesson, she amazed her father—playing the professor—by bursting into real tears.

For years young George Williams sulked in the background while his sister and frantically exuberant brother Adger were in the forefront of the action. I finally settled on using George as the malcontent in any given scene. Then one year he discovered a wig, cane and old coat in the costume pile. He was by then a gawking teenager, but he chose to become a crochety demanding old duffer. Waving his cane at his contemporaries, he shouted, "People didn't do that sort of thing in my day." A permanent character was born into the performing company.

Boys in general were less patient with our ad lib charades, but George's friend, Chris Jenner, enjoyed losing himself in the action and did a fine job as a youth as long as his size permitted. Unfortunately he grew so fast that he soon had to play adult parts.

I could not begin to single out all of the many people who were willing participants. The Blase McCarthys, the Jack Moores and the Tom Tidmores were willing participants. My Nancy has been costume mistress and our daughters Carey, Kathleen and Meg have adapted each year to a variety of roles.

It has been an activity that I shall miss. The stacks of photographs, sketches and prints are a reminder of a time when we were all young together for a few afternoons each year, dressing up and improving the life styles of our ancestors. There will always be something special about members of the "Down Home" family. I hope they will remember our times together as happily as I do.

The work of editing was done by my wife Nancy, Graham Dellinger and Liz McCarthy. I am grateful to them for their patience.

Most of all, I am indebted to the Grizzard Advertising, Inc. for their encouragement and continued use of my services to create the forty prints that are the basis of this book. Grizzard Advertising has been most generous in allowing me to use them. Together with additional sketches and paintings, they are a picture of life in the long afternoon.

John Kollock has been a part of the hills of northeast Georgia all of his life. Except for a tour with the Army in Germany—which gave him the background for helping the people of Helen, Georgia convert their town into an alpine village—he has never been very far from the mountains.

For many years he has worked in commercial art, book illustration and historical writing. Eighteen years ago he began to work in water-colors to capture the rapidly disappearing rural world of his youth. This has led to a number of one man shows each year as well as gallery sales and commissions for special projects, including a painting for the White House. In 1976 his own book, *These Gentle Hills*, was published and after selling out the first edition in three months, it has become a regional classic. His children's book, *Meg's World*, is now in its third printing. Other books on which he has collaborated include *The Winter Folk* and *The Best Friend*.

In recent years he has expanded his painting subject matter to include the fishing villages and marshes of the Georgia and Carolina coasts, as well as the countryside of England and Germany, where he and his wife, Nancy, conduct occasional tours.

111